My Dogs ARE My Babies

Written by: Mary Beth McSweeney

Introduction:

Most pets are considered members of the family. And dogs are considered "Man's Best Friend" for good reason. And using the word "Man" is just general for all humans alike. Dogs can be everyone's best friend and sometimes more than that!

Some dogs have special purposes and are born with innate abilities and given specialized training. These are definitely special dogs, and they include: Police K-9 detective dogs and other specially trained police dogs, dogs for the blind or otherwise disabled, and special therapy dogs, just to name a few...

And some dogs are just very special in their own way. But they are all just as unique as you and me! Yes, dogs have personalities and even face some of the same challenges we do (like anxiety, for one example). And because dogs are so much like us, they understand us to a certain extent, which makes them ideal best friends, since they are so loyal as well.

For me, dogs have always been a necessary part of my life, both before and especially, after disabilities struck. I've always needed an extra pair of eyes and ears to keep me alert at home, and the added safety my dogs provide has been just as important. But the companionship has of course, meant the most.

Since I cannot have children, my dogs always have been and always will be my babies. And some of my dogs have uniquely possessed some of my own characteristics and personality traits.

I will tell you all about all three of my babies: Roxy, Harley and Gnarls.   And I think you will learn why each of them is so important to me that I would consider them my children, not just my best friends.   But dogs are so important to me that I can't bear living without one... or two... ☺

Roxy:

Roxy was truly one of a kind and special in every way possible. When my late husband and I were dating, we rescued Roxy from an uncared for trailer (in Georgia while visiting my husband John's brother who lived in a trailer park); she was the runt of the litter at only four weeks old, and I was glad I took her when I did because Animal Control came to get the mother and remaining pups the next day; so Roxy may have well been the only surviving dog in the bunch (because I insisted that John let me take her home with us).

At only four weeks old, Roxy was tiny enough to fit in the palm of my hand, and she was content to ride between my legs in the car all eight hours of the drive home. Little did I know then that she would always be a dog who loved to go for a ride... but I'll get to that later. When I brought her home, she stayed with me until she was old enough to be trained (by John), and she was so tiny and fragile. She had to be bottle-fed, just like a baby, and I kept her in a crate beside my bed in which she had a heating blanket, water, towels, pee pads and a clock to mimic her mother's heartbeat; and sometimes she got pulled into the bed with me.

And because of her malnutrition and previous neglect after just being born, Roxy was riddled with all kinds of problems, the kind that could've even killed her, like Parvo for example. And my poor baby girl fought hard but remained sick the entire first year of her life, with trips to the vet every week or every other week and expenses piling up (I was grateful to my parents for helping foot the bill) ... But much like me, Roxy was a survivor, and once she survived that first year, she was never sick again until old age.

But before her first year of life was up, the vet approved her for training; and my husband John worked his magic with her. John trained her so well that we never had to worry about her. And she was so well-trained and even-tempered that it seemed as if she understood everything we said... and I guess that's possible since she had only heard English from four weeks old on... I wish I had digital photos of her at that age to share here, but those pictures were taken before the age of digital cameras; and she was so adorable that it really is a shame I can't put a picture with my words!

As Roxy was shuffled back and forth between my husband and I while we were dating, we jokingly referred to her as our "illegitimate child." But Roxy loved the shuffling because that involved riding in the car, which she truly loved to do. In fact, if you asked her, "Do you want to go for a ride?", you couldn't even get out the first few words without her heading to the door, turning in circles all the way, and yipping in excitement. And Roxy certainly knew those words of English because she reacted the same regardless of who asked her about a ride.

But when my husband and I got married and moved in together, Roxy was in her rightful place; and we could no longer joke that she was "illegitimate." Roxy was our child together, and she went everywhere we did. Everyone knew Roxy and everyone loved her, too! She was like the ideal child, doing everything she was told on top of being good all the time. And because life took John from me too soon, Roxy was our only child together (and the only properly trained dog I've owned).

And after John was gone, Roxy attended to me and my special needs. When I was in the hospital, Roxy was brought to me, and that kept me going. Roxy was always a faithful and loyal companion, but she was also very in tune with the situation around her. She knew how to behave, and it was easy for others to care for her in my brief absence. She was both smart and sensitive; and wanting to be with her made me better sooner!

…Oh, that's right… I haven't mentioned her breed or what she looked like since I haven't shown you a picture yet; but the answer will again leave you saying this dog is unique: Roxy was a Boxer mixed with a Corgi. She was all filled out in Boxer muscle and core, but she had the tiny little legs of a Corgi and a face with ears to match. Roxy was unique in both physical appearance and personality. So enough with the suspense… here's one picture of Roxy to give you a visual idea.

Roxy loved everyone; however, she was a very racist dog by nature. She didn't like anyone of color, and sometimes she would be skeptical of a few white people. But she had this thing about people of color. We could be in the car at a stoplight next to a car with a person of a different race in it, and Roxy would bark and growl at the window until our cars pulled away from each other. She was truly racist, and that trait was not taught.

However, her racism didn't apply to children. Roxy loved all children of any age, color or race. She proved this over and over in different situations all the time, and I have two stories as examples of that to share. In the background of the first story, my sister Kelly and her husband and four cats were all living with Roxy and me in order to help me out after disabilities hit.

Kelly was pregnant with my first-born nephew, Ian, and Roxy was very protective of her. But it was after Ian was born that we saw how much Roxy loved children, even babies. Roxy would sit on top of the couch watching over Ian in his crib beside the couch, or she would be underneath the crib – at all times watching over and protecting Ian. And if Ian cried about anything at all, Roxy would alert you to the problem even if you were already taking care of it. Roxy worried every time baby Ian cried, and she remained protective of both Kelly and Ian. She knew they were family...

So we knew how much Roxy loved babies and children, but she proved her racism didn't apply to kids in this next story: After my own recovery and rehabilitation, I felt the need to do something more with my life, and I became a Big Sister with Big Brothers Big Sisters. My new (and very sweet) six-year-old little sister, who was born of color, got together once a week or so for several years. And that sweet little girl begged until she got the chance to spend the night with me, and I was slightly worried about how Roxy would react to her…

But Roxy adored her, no reaction to color whatsoever, and we all became family together, with Roxy right in the middle of things. And Roxy was there for my little sister's big events (like birthday parties), too; and Roxy didn't mind taking this next picture at one of those parties for my little sister:

Roxy enjoyed being an only child and getting all the attention, and I wondered if she would get along with a sibling dog. I'll continue that thought in my next chapter about her sibling, Harley. But for now, we bring Roxy's story to a close. She was with me from infancy until age seventeen, when she suffered from her second stroke and for her own sake, had to be put to sleep. That broke my heart, and the loss was tragic for me... from several aspects... But she is in Heaven with her daddy now, forever happy. ☺

Roxy brought me so much joy for so many years of my life, and she saw me through some really hard times. She was my baby, and yet, she took care of me. I mothered her from the beginning of her life right up to the end, and she was the best dog ever! But like I said, her story doesn't end here because she gets a sister before old age really comes! And that changes things...

Harley:

Roxy was several years old (but certainly not an old dog and definitely still learning new tricks) when her sister Harley came along and changed our world together – but for the better. Of course, it took Roxy a few days to deal with the overbearing puppy that Harley was, but she finally accepted her as a sister, and we became a big, happy family.

So it's time to tell you all about Harley, a special dog in her own way. My best friend brought Harley to my house (because she couldn't keep her) after rescuing her from the pound at just three and a half months old. And like Roxy, Harley had also been abused and neglected in her short life before coming to me. Long story short, Harley ended up staying with me and Roxy that day and from there on...

Harley was a black Lab mixed with Border Collie, and she was full of energy but a little clumsy as a puppy with her long legs (the proof is in the next picture I'll show you of how Harley looked when she came to me). And besides energy, Harley was full of love! Even after her abusive past, she loved everyone and was genuinely excited to see people she knew. For example, when family or friends she knew well would come to visit, she would greet them at the door and get so excited to see them that she'd pee all over the floor. She couldn't seem to hold in her excitement or her pee!

Harley may have been taller and larger than Roxy (in life but even as a puppy this was true...), but she regarded Roxy with great respect and loved her older sister instantly (not that the feeling was instant for Roxy). Harley learned almost everything she knew from Roxy, so Roxy kind of helped me train this new pup.

Roxy had to help me train Harley because John was no longer around to work his magic, and Harley was a big handful for me;

and with so little training in comparison to Roxy, Harley was more mischievous and in that way, more like "my" child. But Harley was always the first one to take the blame for any mischief; even if Roxy was the one at fault, Harley would bow her head and act as if she was the trouble-maker and be genuinely sorry for it. She was just so sweet even when she was trouble...

For one thing, Harley was an escape-artist. She would dig a hole under the backyard fence, climb under and out to wherever she wanted (usually somewhere in the neighborhood). And I can't even count how many times that happened, times when she would leave me worried for a day or two before neighbors called me to get her if I couldn't find her first. And even when my dad helped me blockade the fence, Harley would still find a way out. She loved home but was always wanting to explore...

But for any trouble Harley was, she was also mostly obedient; and she always had the sweetest nature, the most loving soul. Except for her jumping habit, everyone loved Harley (just not the scratches on their legs from her excitement to see them).

Harley came to me riddled with anxiety issues, especially over sirens, loud noises and storms. Now, Roxy never howled a day in her life, but Harley howled at every siren she heard. And during storms, Harley would find a place to hide and cower; and she would shake and shed all over the place.

Harley basically had two different looks/hairstyles, full hair or shaved. And it made her look like two different dogs:

…So Roxy helped train Harley when she came along; and many years later when Roxy was old and having a hard time getting around, Harley would stay with Roxy, looking after her big sister.

Those two really became close sisters, and they both took care of each other and me as much as I ever took care of them! Here's a few pictures of my girls together:

As I said, Harley looked out for Roxy when she needed it. And Harley was so concerned when Roxy had her first and second strokes a couple of years apart. Harley stayed by Roxy's side and cared for her in every way she could. After Roxy passed away, Harley grieved with me, and I was grateful for the company as Harley then stayed by my side as she had done with Roxy. Their final picture shows Harley not even leaving Roxy's remains, sister's to the end.

Harley stayed with me, always loving, loyal and sweet as she naturally was, for three more years after Roxy died. Harley died suddenly and certainly unexpected at the age of eight; but I was with her till her last breath. It tore me apart to see her in pain that I couldn't help; I felt truly helpless when I lost Harley, and the dangers of depression quickly set in for me. But the same best friend of mine that brought me Harley came to rescue me in the form of rescuing another dog – and I'm glad my friend came quickly! And I'm glad Harley is with Roxy again in Heaven...

Gnarls

My friend took me to the pound and then to the Nashville Humane Society, where I found Gnarls, or rather, Gnarls found me! He had been named "Little Man" because of his size (even though he was already two and a half years old), and he was so small and shaking and scared that he wouldn't let anyone else at the Society touch him… but when I went inside his room with him and sat down, he came to me – and it was like it was meant to be, special from the start!!!

Needless to say, I adopted this sweet boy and renamed him Gnarls, because that seemed to better suit him (little did I know...). My best friend made sure I had everything I needed to take care of a tiny dog; and on that day, Gnarls loved us both... but after my friend went home, Gnarls claimed me! He was so comfortable with me, which I thought was special since I saw him shy away from so many others. He's my special Little Man now appropriately named Gnarls (my Gnarly boy).

Gnarls was also previously abused and neglected, and he has a term called "Defensive Aggression," bless his sweet heart... He only trusts me – no one else! In fact, he sees everyone and everything else as a threat; and he is always extra protective of me. So everyone else gets gnarls, growls and lots of barking, if not also aggressive behavior. No one gets to see how sweet he is with me – it's like Gnarls is two different dogs.

And I spoiled Gnarls from the beginning, giving him lots of love, play, toys and treats – and this boy loves his toys and especially treats! He was not trained well by me (due to my own circumstances), and no one who wants to interact with him can, because again, he only loves and trusts me. In addition, he doesn't get enough exercise to compensate for all the treats, so he's gained a lot of weight in the time that I've owned him.

Gnarls is not in any way social, nor does he like to be; but secretly, he wants to be… he just doesn't know how… So most people are leery of him, and I don't blame them; and others just put up with his barking from the cage (where he can't try to bite any ankles). I guess I say all this to emphasize that he only loves me, is protective, but is also the lover-boy that nobody else gets to see!

Gnarls is a funny, quirky boy about a lot of things: For example, he just loves to go in the bathroom and mess up my rugs; I find them in a mess multiple times daily… Another example is how he has OCD about the placement of certain toys; they all have to be where he wants them, and if I move them, he gets disturbed and immediately puts them back – my boy does know what he wants. Finally, Gnarls is obsessed with getting under the covers in the bed.

As I said before, my boy Gnarls loves getting loves and as many treats as possible. But he does the sweetest thing when he wants something... he has a little "begging foot" as I like to call it. See:

Well, in truth, we both need love as well as have anxiety issues; but we complement each other well. He may not be trained, but he is my own personal therapy dog – and I depend on him for a lot of things! Gnarls alone is my extra pair of eyes and ears; he is my valiant protector; his is my sweet little man, my only baby boy, and my best friend. I call him my Prince Gnarls because he is like royalty to me, and he tends to "ride in on his white horse" and save me when I need it. Oh, my sweet Gnarly boy...

Above all, Gnarls is my favorite cuddle-buddy ever! I've never had a snuggle buddy like him before. We love bedtime (both at night and naps) together, but the best part of every day we call "TV/Cuddle-Time". I've always loved watching shows on TV, but Gnarls brings this time of day to a new level... the best part of TV/Cuddle-Time are the cuddles and loves!!!

And we both enjoy watching Nashville Predators play hockey because game time makes for lots of cuddles. I've been a Predators fan from the start, and now Gnarls has joined me. Since he isn't a social dog, I could never really get him to dress up and go anywhere. Watching together at home is fun because when I get excited about a goal, Gnarls jumps up too. But like I said, the games make for great cuddle-times! And someone special to me made a card with the next picture on it that made my day!!!

GO PREDS!

Conclusion:

Appreciate your dogs or find one to love and appreciate. And be a responsible owner to every extent that you can. Consider your dog as your baby or best friend, if for nothing else than their unconditional love and loyalty. They are most definitely members of the family, whether you want to call them that or not; and sometimes, they're the easiest of all family members to love...

Not all dogs are friendly, and some have been abused or neglected enough to be mean. But most of those dogs are just misunderstood, like Gnarls, for instance. He appears to be fierce and shows aggression towards others, and yet, he is one of the most loving, sweetest dogs I've known – so misunderstood!

And have some respect for the dogs that do perform special services, usually requiring the training to go with it. But let's give all dogs a little more respect for the love, loyalty, comfort and many other services that all of them provide – all dogs are special. And yes, I feel quite sure all dogs really do go to Heaven because their souls are just as precious as our own.

The End